THE BIG BOOK OF
SILLY JOKES
FOR KIDS

The Big Book of

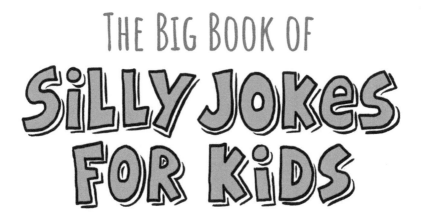

Silly Jokes For Kids

800+ Knock-Knocks, Tongue Twisters, Silly Stats, and More!

By Carole P. Roman

Illustrations by
Dylan Goldberger

ROCKRIDGE
PRESS

Art Director: Eric Pratt
Art Manager: Sue Bischofberger
Editor: Erin Nelson
Production Editor: Erum Khan
Illustrations © Dylan Goldberger, 2019 | dylangoldberger.com
ISBN: Print 978-1-64152-637-1 | eBook: 978-1-64611-355-2

To my dad.
He always knew
how to lighten
any situation
with a good joke.

LAUGHTER

is The Shortest Distance Between Two People.

—Victor Borge

Contents

Howdy, jokester!

Sometimes big laughs come in small packages. While *The Big Book of Silly Jokes for Kids* is something you can hold in one hand or pop into your backpack, it's also something I hope will give you laughs for years to come.

I wrote this book thinking of the fun you and your family might share after a long day. Many of these jokes have become staples in my own family, making everyone from grandkid to grandma giggle with glee. We are all so busy that the simple pleasure of exchanging a funny story, or having a rapid-fire pun contest is something special I wanted to celebrate in these pages.

So, whether you are looking to give your friends a knee-slapper with a knock-knock joke, stump a grown-up with a riddle, practice your comedian skills with a tricky tongue twister, or chuckle quietly to a run of jokes in your room, this book is meant for you . . . and all of your funny bones.

HA! Q&A

No matter where we live or what language we speak, one of the most important things we have in common is humor. When people laugh at a joke, many of our differences disappear.

Jokes can be a single question or even a story. What makes a joke so funny? Jokes surprise us with unexpected twists. They get us to look closely at words and figure out what they mean. When we suddenly get it, the surprise tickles our funny bone.

Many jokes have been told and retold so often that we don't know who actually thought of them. They belong to us all. Can you think of the last funny joke you heard? It's your joke to tell now!

You know how to laugh and make others laugh, so let's get to some joke cracking.

What's a pirate's favorite letter of the alphabet?

ARRRRGH!

Who's the queen of the pencil case?

The ruler.

What time do you go to the dentist?

Tooth-hurty.

What did the nose say to the finger?

"Quit picking on me!"

Silly Stat: Just like fingerprints, tooth prints are unique to each person. They are as individual as you are!

What did the left eye say to the right eye?

"Between us, something smells."

How do you make a tissue dance?

You put a little boogie in it.

What time is it when the clock strikes 13?

Time to get a new clock.

How do we know that the ocean is friendly?

It waves!

Why did the kid cross the playground?

To get to the other slide.

What is a tornado's favorite game to play?

Twister.

What falls in winter but never gets hurt?

Snow!

When does a joke become a "dad" joke?

When the punchline is a parent.

How do you stop an astronaut's baby from crying?

You rocket!

How are false teeth like stars?

They come out at night!

Why couldn't the astronaut book a hotel on the moon?

Because it was full.

Silly Stat: The distance from the moon to the earth is about roughly 238,900 miles. It takes about three days to travel from the earth to the moon.

How does the moon cut his hair?

Eclipse it.

What did the man say when he walked into a bar?

"Ouch!"

What has four wheels and flies?

A garbage truck.

How do you throw a party in space?

You planet.

What are the strongest days of the week?

Saturday and Sunday. Every other day is a weak day.

Why are robots never afraid?
They have nerves of steel.

Why are pirates, pirates?
Because they just arrrrgh!

**Why did the kid bring
a ladder to school?**
Because she wanted
to go to high school.

**What did one ocean
say to another ocean
when it asked the
other out on a date?**
"Shore."

**Why are shoemakers
such kind people?**
Because they have
good soles.

**Why did the kid
bury the battery?**
Because it was dead.

**Why couldn't the pirate
learn the alphabet?**
Because he was
always lost at "c."

What do elves learn in school?

The elf-abet.

Where do pencils go on vacation?

Pencil-vania.

What building in New York has the most stories?

The public library.

What did the tween give his mom?

Ughs and kisses!

Why was the student's report card wet?

Because it was below "C" level.

What did one volcano say to the other?

"I lava you!"

Why didn't the dog want to play football?

It was a boxer!

What musical instrument is found in the bathroom?

A tuba toothpaste.

What did the big flower say to the little flower?

"Hi, bud!"

Kid: What are you doing under there?

Mom: Under where?
Kid: Ha! You said underwear!

Which flower will tell all your secrets?

Tulips.

What do you call a funny mountain?

Hill-arious.

What gets wetter the more it dries?

A towel.

What's brown, has no legs, but has a head and tail?

A penny.

Silly Stat: Pennies were one of the first coins minted in the United States. Do you know which American president's head is on the penny? (*Hint:* He was very tall!)

What did the book put on when it was cold?

A jacket.

Why did the man put his money in the freezer?

He wanted cold, hard cash.

How did the phone propose to its girlfriend?

It gave her a ring.

What did the painter say to her sweetheart?

"I love you with all my art."

What did one snowman say to another snowman?
"You're cool."

Why is there a gate around cemeteries?

Because people are dying to get in!

What stays in the corner yet can travel all over the world?

A stamp.

What do planets like to read?

Comet books.

What do you call an older snowman?

Water.

What do lawyers wear to court?

Lawsuits.

What has one head, one foot, and four legs?

A bed.

Why does Humpty Dumpty love autumn?
Because he always has a great fall.

**What word is always
spelled wrong in
the dictionary?**
Wrong.

**What did one snowman
say to the other snowman?**
"Wanna chill?"

**What do snowmen take
when the sun gets too hot?**
A chill pill.

**Why did the scarecrow
win an award?**
She was the best in her field.

**Where does a snowman
keep his money?**
In a snowbank.

**What kind of award did
the dentist receive?**
A little plaque.

**What kind of ball
doesn't bounce?**
A snowball.

**Why was the little
boy so cold?**
Because it was
Decembrrrrr!

What is the coldest country in the world?

Chile.

What has a bow but can't be tied?

A rainbow.

What is the best day to go to the beach?

Sunday.

What did the picture say to the wall?

"Do you mind if I hang around?"

What else did the picture say to the wall?

"Help! I've been framed."

What's the best season to jump on a trampoline?

Spring time.

Why did the girl go to bed with a pen?

To draw the curtains.

Why is dark spelled with a "k" and not a "c?"

Because you can't "c" in the dark.

How do you make fire with two sticks?

Make sure they are a match!

What's a balloon's least favorite type of music?

Pop.

Silly Stat: The trampoline was introduced to the public in Central Park, New York City, with a kangaroo jumping on it.

Why were they called the Dark Ages?

Because there were lots of knights.

Which rock group has four guys who can't sing or play instruments?

Mount Rushmore.

Want to hear a roof joke?

The first one's on the house.

How do hair stylists speed up their job?

They take shortcuts.

What did the goat ask for at the barbershop?

"A goatee trim for me!"

Silly Stat: Did you know the barbershop was an important part of the American civil rights movement? The barbershop was a place for community members to get together, share news, and spread the word.

Who can shave six times a day and still have a beard?

A barber.

What has only one eye, but still can't see?

A needle.

Why was the broom late?

It over-swept.

What starts and ends with "e" but has only one letter in it?

Envelope.

Where can you always find a tiger's head?

A few feet from its tail.

Where do sheep go on vacation?

To the Baaaaaahamas.

What can you catch but never throw?

A cold.

What animal is best at hitting a baseball?

A bat.

What did the girlfriend say to the billy goat?

"You have goat to be kidding me."

What runs around a baseball field but never moves?

The fence.

What did the baseball glove say to the ball?

"Catch you later."

What did the football coach say to the broken vending machine?

"I want my quarterback!"

I couldn't figure out why the baseball kept getting bigger . . .

Then it hit me.

What do you call a secret group of llamas?

The I-llama-nati (*Illuminati*).

What did the llama say to the sad camel?
"Don't worry, you'll get over this hump."

What's more amazing than a talking llama?
A spelling bee!

How is a baseball team similar to a pancake?
They both need a good batter.

Why is a baseball stadium always cool?
It is full of fans.

When is a baseball player like a spider?
When he catches a fly!

Why do basketball players love doughnuts?
Because they can dunk 'em!

Why did the golfer wear two pairs of pants?
In case she got a hole-in-one.

What did the astronaut say when he crashed into the moon?
"I Apollo-gize."

What has 18 legs and catches flies?
A baseball team.

What kinds of stories do volleyball players tell?
Tall tales!

What is harder to catch the faster you run?
Your breath.

You know what's odd?
Every other number!

How can you tell if a plant is a math plant?
Because of its square roots.

**What is a bird's favorite
type of math?**
Owl-gebra.

**Why did the two fours
not want any dinner?**
Because they already eight!

Why is six afraid of seven?
Because seven ate nine.

**What did the zero
say to the eight?**
"Nice belt."

**Why was the math
book unhappy?**
Because it had too
many problems!

**What did the triangle
say to the circle?**
"You're pointless."

**How do you make seven
an even number?**
Remove the "s."

**Why did the obtuse
angle go to the beach?**
Because it was
over 90 degrees.

Why was the math lesson so long?

Because the teacher kept going off on a tangent.

What did the mother angle say to her baby?

"Aww, what acute angle."

Silly Stat: Irish immigrants brought the tradition of carving jack-o'-lanterns to America. However, in Ireland, they used potatoes and turnips.

Why shouldn't you argue with a decimal?

Because decimals always have a point.

Why should you not talk to pi?

Because it will go on forever.

What do you get when you divide the circumference of a jack-o'-lantern by its diameter?

Pumpkin pi!

Want me to tell you a joke about pizza?

Sorry, it's too cheesy.

Why did the girl toss a stick of butter?

She wanted to see a butterfly.

What do you call cheese that isn't yours?

Nacho cheese.

What is a smartphone's favorite snack?

Computer chips!

What kind of tree fits in your hand?
A palm tree.

What is fast, loud, and crunchy?
A rocket chip!

Why did the student eat her homework?
Because the teacher said it was a piece of cake.

What has ears but cannot hear?
A cornfield.

What did one plate say to the other plate?
"Dinner is on me."

What's the worst vegetable to have on a ship?
A leek.

How do pickles enjoy a day out?
They relish it.

What room can you never enter?
A mushroom.

**What did the cucumber
say to the pickle?**
"You mean a great
dill to me."

**What do you call two
banana peels?**
Slippers.

**Why didn't the orange
win the race?**
It ran out of juice.

**Why do bananas put
on suntan lotion?**
Because they don't
want to peel.

**Why did the cookie
go to the doctor?**
Because he felt crummy.

**Why did the banana
go to the doctor?**
Because it wasn't
peeling well.

Why did the tomato blush?

Because it saw the salad dressing.

Why did the lettuce win the race?

Because it was a head.

When do you stop at green and go at red?

When you're eating a watermelon.

Why didn't the robot finish his breakfast?

Because the orange juice told him to concentrate.

Why did Mozart sell his chickens?

They kept saying, "Bach, Bach, Bach."

What did the hamburger give her sweetheart?

An onion ring.

How do you fix a cracked jack-o'-lantern?

Give it a pumpkin patch.

What fruit do scarecrows love the most?

Strawberries.

How do ghosts wash their hair?

With sham-boo!

What is a ghost's favorite dessert?

I scream.

What kinds of pants do ghosts wear?

Boo jeans.

What room does a ghost not use?

A living room.

What do you call a snake in a bakery?

A pie-thon.

**What do you call a
ghost's true love?**

Their ghoul-friend.

**Where do baby ghosts
go during the day?**

To day-scare centers!

**What is a ghost's
nose full of?**

Boooooo-gers!

Why are ghosts bad liars?

Because you can see
right through them.

**Why didn't the
skeleton take his
friend to the prom?**

His heart wasn't in it.

**Why didn't the skeleton
cross the road?**

Because he didn't
have the guts.

**Why didn't the skeleton
go to the dance?**

He had no body
to dance with.

**What do you call a witch
who goes to the beach?**

A sand-witch.

**What is a witch's favorite
subject in school?**

Spelling.

**What do you call two
witches who live together?**

Broom-mates.

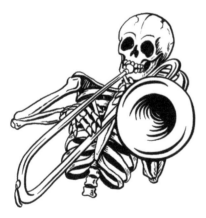

**What instrument does
a skeleton play?**

The trombone.

What do birds say on Halloween?
"Trick or tweet!"

**What do vampires
give you in winter?**
Frostbite!

**What monster is
the best artist?**
Dracula, because he
likes to draw blood.

**How can you tell a
vampire has a cold?**
He starts coffin.

**What monster plays
tricks on Halloween?**
Prank-enstein!

**What is a vampire's
favorite fruit?**
A blood orange.

**What kind of music
do mummies love?**
Wrap music.

**How does a vampire
start a letter?**
Tomb it may concern...

**What did the farmer
give his family for
Valentine's Day?**
Hogs and kisses.

What did the stamp say to the envelope on Valentine's Day?

"I'm stuck on you."

Why do skunks love Valentine's Day?

They are very scent-imental creatures.

What did one lightbulb say to the other lightbulb?

"I wuv you watts and watts!"

What do you write in a slug's Valentine's Day card?

Be my valen-slime.

What happened when the Easter bunny didn't behave in school?

He was egg-spelled.

Why do mummies like birthdays so much?

Because of all the wrapping!

Which is the best hand to light the Hanukkah menorah?

Neither. It's best to use a candle.

What do you call a greedy elf?

Elfish.

What do you say to an octopus on Valentine's Day?

"I want to hold your hand, hand, hand, hand, hand, hand, hand, hand!"

Why do bees hum?

Because they don't know the words.

What is a cow's favorite holiday?
Moo Year's Day.

**What comes at the end
of Christmas Day?**
The letter "y."

**What did the
gingerbread man put
under his blankets?**
A cookie sheet.

**What do you call Santa
when he stops moving?**
Santa Pause.

**What should you never
eat on July 4th?**
Firecrackers.

What do you call an alligator wearing a vest?
An investigator.

What do you call a sleeping dinosaur?
A dino-snore.

Why don't dinosaurs eat clowns?
Because they taste funny.

What do owls say to declare their love?
"Owl be yours."

Why does a seagull fly over the sea?
Because if it flew over the bay, it would be a bay-gull.

Why don't koalas count as bears?
They don't have the right koala-fications.

Why do bees have sticky hair?
Because they use a honeycomb.

What kind of haircuts do bees get?
Buzzzzz cuts.

What did the bee say to the flower?
"Hi, honey."

**What did one bee
say to the other?**

"I love bee-ing with you."

**What do you call
a clever bee?**

A spelling bee.

**What's worse than finding
a worm in your apple?**

Finding half a worm.

**Why did the ants
dance on the jam jar?**

Because the lid said,
"Twist to open."

**What do you get when
you cross a centipede
with a parrot?**

A walkie-talkie.

**How do you know
a squirrel has had
too much candy?**

It's acting like a nut.

**What do you call a
bear that jumps but
never lands?**

Peter Panda.

**What do you get when
you cross an elephant
and a potato?**

Mashed potatoes.

**What do you call
two birds in love?**

Tweet-hearts.

**What do you get
when you cross an
elephant with a fish?**

Swimming trunks.

**What kind of pillar can't
hold up a building?**

A caterpillar.

What time is it when an elephant sits on your fence?
Time to get a new fence.

Silly Stat: Did you know that elephants can't jump? But they're not the only ones. Rhinoceroses, hippopotamuses, and sloths can't jump either.

Where would you find an elephant?
The same place that you lost her.

Where do elephants pack their clothes?
In their trunks.

How do you stop an elephant from charging?
Take away his credit card.

What did the wolf say when it stubbed its toe?
"Howwwwwl!"

How do you know that carrots are good for your eyesight?

Have you ever seen a rabbit with glasses?

What kind of shoes do frogs wear?

Open toad shoes.

Why did the chewing gum cross the road?

It was stuck to the chicken's foot.

Why do farmers put bells on cows?

Their horns don't make noise.

What do dogs do when watching Netflix?

They press paws.

What did the banana say to the dog?

Nothing. Bananas can't talk.

Why aren't dogs good dancers?

They have two left feet.

What kind of key can never unlock a door?

A monkey.

What goes *tick-tock* and *woof-woof*?

A watchdog.

What do you call a monkey that loves potato chips?

A chip-monk.

What happened when the skunk was on trial?

The judge declared, "Odor in the court, odor in the court!"

What do you get when you cross a dog with a telephone?

A golden receiver.

Where do dogs park?

In a barking lot.

What did the Dalmatian say after lunch?

"That hit the spot."

What do you call a sleeping bull?

A bulldozer.

Why can't you play hockey with pigs?

They always hog the puck.

Why do porcupines always win the game?

They have the most points.

What do you call a bear with no teeth?

A gummy bear.

Why did the teddy bear say "no" to dessert?

Because he was stuffed.

What do you call a pig that knows karate?

Pork chop.

What do you call a duck that gets all "A's"?

A wise-quacker.

How do you make a jellyfish laugh?

With ten-tickles!

Silly Stat: A common mistake is to think an octopus has tentacles. Scientifically speaking, an octopus has eight arms and zero tentacles!

Why wouldn't the crab share his treasure?

Because he was a little shellfish.

Why did they quit giving tests at the zoo?

Because it was full of cheetahs.

Why couldn't the pony sing a lullaby?

She was a little hoarse.

**What do you call a fish
without an eye?**

A fssssssh.

**How many South
Americans does it take
to change a lightbulb?**

A Brazilian.

**Why was there thunder
and lightning in the lab?**

They were brainstorming.

**Why did the tree go
to the dentist?**

To get a root canal.

**What goes up and down
but doesn't move?**

Stairs.

**What do you call
a dog magician?**

A Labra-ca-dabra-dor.

**What's black and white
and red all over?**

An embarrassed zebra.

**Why did the police officer
go to the baseball game?**

She heard someone
had stolen a base.

**What kind of car does
Mickey Mouse's
girlfriend drive?**

A Minnie van.

**What do you call
a happy cowboy?**

A jolly rancher.

**Why couldn't the
pirate play cards?**

Because he was
sitting on the deck.

What letters are not in the alphabet?

The ones in the mail.

Why do fish live in saltwater?

Because pepper makes them sneeze.

How does a train eat?

It goes chew-chew.

Where do young cows eat lunch?

In the calf-eteria.

What type of markets do dogs avoid?

Flea markets.

What's a cat's favorite color?

Purrr-ple.

How do you make gold soup?

Put 24 carrots in it.

What time do ducks wake up?

At the quack of dawn.

What kind of bird works at a construction site?

A crane.

KNOCK, KNOCK

Can you think back to the first joke you ever told? There is a good chance it was a knock-knock joke. You might even feel like you were born knowing how to knock, knock.

Knock-knock jokes first became popular in America in the 1920s, but they are told all over the world. In French, the joke starts with "toc, toc." In Afrikaans and Dutch, it's "klop, klop." In Korean and Japanese, it's "kon, kon." And in Spanish, knock-knock jokes often rhyme!

Knock-knock jokes are fun because they always follow the same format. Most of them are short and easy to remember. In fact, once you start doing them, it's hard to stop!

Knock, knock.
Who's there?
You.
You who?
Yoo-hoo, it's your turn!

Knock, knock.
Who's there?
Aardvark.
Aardvark who?
**Aardvark a hundred miles
for you.**

Knock, knock.
Who's there?
Honey bee.
Honey bee who?
Honey bee good!

Silly Stat: Did you know that insects are considered a good source of nutrition for some animals, even humans? Most of them are rich in protein, healthy fats, iron, and calcium, and low in carbohydrates. Many countries include insects as an essential part of their daily diet. What bugs would you be willing to try?

Knock, knock.
Who's there?
Alli.
Alli who?
Alligator.

Knock, knock.
Who's there?
A herd.
A herd who?
**A herd you were home,
so I came over.**

Knock, knock.
Who's there?
Lion.
Lion who?
Lion bed, sleepyhead.

Knock, knock.
Who's there?
Cow-go.
Cow-go who?
Cow-go, "Moo, moo."

Knock, knock.
Who's there?
Ruff.
Ruff who?
Ruff, ruff, it's your dog.

Knock, knock.
Who's there?
Thumpin'.
Thumpin' who?
**There's thumpin' furry
crawling up your back.**

Knock, knock.
Who's there?
Doughnut.
Doughnut who?
**Doughnut leave before
you walk the dog.**

Knock, knock.
Who's there?
Chick.
Chick who?
**Chick your shoelaces,
they're untied.**

Knock, knock.
Who's there?
Iguana.
Iguana who?
Iguana hold your hand.

Knock, knock.
Who's there?
Alpaca.
Alpaca who?
**Alpaca suitcase,
you pack a lunch!**

Knock, knock.
Who's there?
Owl.
Owl who?
**Owl-gebra class
is my favorite!**

Knock, knock.
Who's there?
Moose.
Moose who?
**Moose you tell these
knock-knock jokes?**

Knock, knock.
Who's there?
Giraffe.
Giraffe who?
Giraffe anything to eat?
I'm hungry.

Knock, knock.
Who's there?
Owls.
Owls who?
Why yes, they do.

Knock, knock.
Who's there?
Moo.
Moo who?
Aww, don't cry, baby calf.

Knock, knock.
Who's there?
Toucan.
Toucan who?
Toucan play that game.

Knock, knock.
Who's there?
Viper.
Viper who?
Viper nose, it's running.

Knock, knock.
Who's there?
Beats.
Beats who?
Beats me.

Knock, knock.
Who's there?
Ice cream.
Ice cream who?
Ice cream with happiness!

Knock, knock.
Who's there?
Cash.
Cash who?
**No thanks, I want
almonds.**

Knock, knock.
Who's there?
Lettuce.
Lettuce who?
**Lettuce in, it's cold
out here!**

Knock, knock.
Who's there?
Eggs.
Eggs who?
Egg-cited to see you.

Knock, knock.
Who's there?
Mustard.
Mustard who?
Mustard you knocking.

Knock, knock.
Who's there?
Broccoli.
Broccoli who?
**Broccoli doesn't have
a last name, silly!**

Knock, knock.
Who's there?
Pecan.
Pecan who?
**Pecan somebody
your own size.**

Knock, knock.
Who's there?
Math.
Math who?
**Can you pass the
math potatoes?**

Knock, knock.
Who's there?
Yam.
Yam who?
I yam what I am.

Knock, knock.
Who's there?
Doughnut.
Doughnut who?
**Doughnut ask where
the treasure is!**
It's a secret.

Knock, knock.
Who's there?
Soup.
Soup who?
Souperwoman!

Knock, knock.
Who's there?
Bean.
Bean who?
Bean there, done that.

Knock, knock.
Who's there?
Seed.
Seed who?
Seed you tomorrow.

Knock, knock.
Who's there?
Olive.
Olive who?
Olive you a lot.

Knock, knock.
Who's there?
Jello.
Jello who?
Jello, is anybody home?

Knock, knock.
Who's there?
Poodle.
Poodle who?
Poodle little ketchup on my burger.

Knock, knock.
Who's there?
Barbie.
Barbie who?
Barbie Q. Chicken.

Knock, knock.
Who's there?
Pete.
Pete who?
Pete-za delivery.

Knock, knock.
Who's there?
Pasta.
Pasta who?
Pasta salt, please.

Silly Stat: In 2005, scientists found a four-thousand-year-old bowl of pasta in China. The long, thin yellow noodles were buried 10 feet below ground and made from two different kinds of millet, a tasty grain!

Knock, knock.
Who's there?
Bunny.
Bunny who?
Some bunny been eating my carrots.

Knock, knock.
Who's there?
Plato.
Plato who?
Plato fish and chips.

Knock, knock.
Who's there?
Peas.
Peas who?
Peas pass the butter.

Knock, knock.
Who's there?
Handsome.
Handsome who?
Handsome mustard to me, please.

Knock, knock.
Who's there?
Noah.
Noah who?
Noah good restaurant around here?

Knock, knock.
Who's there?
Turnip.
Turnip who?
Turnip the music!

Knock, knock.
Who's there?
Nacho.
Nacho who?
**That's nacho sandwich.
It's mine!**

Knock, knock.
Who's there?
Cereal.
Cereal who?
**Cereal pleasure
to meet you.**

Silly Stat: Did you know
that November 6th is
National Nacho Day? Mark
your calendar and dig in to
your favorite cheesy snack.

Knock, knock.
Who's there?
Ketchup.
Ketchup who?
**Ketchup with me
and I'll tell you!**

Knock, knock.
Who's there?
Theresa.
Theresa who?
Theresa fly in my soup.

Knock, knock.
Who's there?
Figs.
Figs who?
**Figs the doorbell, please.
It's broken.**

Knock, knock.
Who's there?
Butter.
Butter who?
Butter let me in soon.

Knock, knock.
Who's there?
Four eggs.
Four eggs who?
Four eggs-ample, it's me.

Knock, knock.
Who's there?
Cheese.
Cheese who?
Cheese such a sweet girl.

Knock, knock.
Who's there?
Dee.
Dee who?
**Dee-licious cookies
for sale.**

Knock, knock.
Who's there?
Orange.
Orange who?
**Orange you gonna
let me in?**

> **Silly Stat:** A bunch of
> bananas are called a hand.

Knock, knock.
Who's there?
Banana.
Banana who?
Knock, knock.
Who's there?
Banana.
Banana who?
Knock, knock.
Who's there?
Orange.
Orange who?
**Orange you glad
I didn't say banana?**

Knock, knock.
Who's there?
Berry.
Berry who?
Berry nice to meet you.

Knock, knock.
Who's there?
Abby.
Abby who?
Abby birthday to you!

Knock, knock.
Who's there?
Jamal.
Jamal who?
Jamal shook up.

Knock, knock.
Who's there?
Ada.
Ada who?
Ada sandwich for lunch.

Knock, knock.
Who's there?
Abby.
Abby who?
A, B, C, D, E, F, G.

Knock, knock.
Who's there?
Alfie.
Alfie who?
Alfie good about the test.

Knock, knock.
Who's there?
Zoom.
Zoom who?
Zoom do you think it is?

Knock, knock.
Who's there?
Alma.
Alma who?
Alma not going to say.

Knock, knock.
Who's there?
Annie.
Annie who?
**Annie body going
to the park?**

Knock, knock.
Who's there?
Spell.
Spell who?
Okay, okay: W-H-O.

Knock, knock.
Who's there?
Abel.
Abel who?
**Abel to leap tall buildings
in a single bound!**

Knock, knock.
Who's there?
Kanga.
Kanga who?
Actually, it's kangaroo.

Knock, knock.
Who's there?
Albert.
Albert who?
**Albert you can't guess
who I am.**

Knock, knock.
Who's there?
Alex.
Alex who?
**Alex the questions
around here.**

Knock, knock.
Who's there?
Alice.
Alice who?
Alice fair in love and war.

Knock, knock.
Who's there?
Dwayne.
Dwayne who?
**Dwayne the bathtub,
it's overflowing.**

Knock, knock.
Who's there?
Andrew.
Andrew who?
**Andrew a nice picture
for you.**

Knock, knock!
Who's there?
Candy.
Candy who?
**Candy cow really jump
over the moon?**

Knock, knock.
Who's there?
Annie.
Annie who?
Annie body home?

Knock, knock.
Who's there?
Annie.
Annie who?
**Annie more of these
knock-knock jokes?**

Knock, knock.
Who's there?
Annetta.
Annetta who?
**Annetta
knock-knock joke.**

Knock, knock.
Who's there?
Muffin.
Muffin who?
**Muffin the matter with
me, how about you?**

Knock, knock.
Who's there?
Barry.
Barry who?
Barry nice to see you.

Knock, knock.
Who's there?
Ben.
Ben who?
Ben there, done that.

Knock, knock.
Who's there?
Carmen.
Carmen who?
Carmen get it.

Knock, knock.
Who's there?
Colin.
Colin who?
**Colin all kids
to get some pasta!**

Knock, knock.
Who's there?
Constance.
Constance who?
**Constance waiting out
here anymore.**

Knock, knock.
Who's there?
Adore.
Adore who?
**Adore is between us.
Open up!**

Knock, knock.
Who's there?
Emma.
Emma who?
**Emma getting hungry.
When's dinner?**

Knock, knock.
Who's there?
Dawn.
Dawn who?
**Dawn forget your
backpack.**

Knock, knock.
Who's there?
Fanny.
Fanny who?
**Fanny body calls,
please tell them I'm out.**

Knock, knock.
Who's there?
Doris.
Doris who?
**Doris a bit squeaky,
do you have some oil?**

Knock, knock.
Who's there?
Fred.
Fred who?
**Who is a Fred of
the big bad wolf?**

Knock, knock.
Who's there?
Freddy.
Freddy who?
**Freddy or not,
here I come!**

Knock, knock.
Who's there?
Gus.
Gus who?
**That's what *you're*
supposed to do!**

Knock, knock.
Who's there?
Gwen.
Gwen who?
Gwen will I see you again?

Knock, knock.
Who's there?
Hal.
Hal who?
Hal-o, anybody home?

Knock, knock.
Who's there?
Frank.
Frank who?
**Frank you for answering
the door.**

Knock, knock.
Who's there?
Harry.
Harry who?
Harry up, I want to go
to the beach!

Knock, knock.
Who's there?
Isabel.
Isabel who?
Isabel necessary
for this door?

Knock, knock.
Who's there?
Howard.
Howard who?
Howard I know?

Knock, knock.
Who's there?
Iris.
Iris who?
Iris you'd sing me a song.

Knock, knock.
Who's there?
Hugh.
Hugh who?
Hugh-who!
Don't you see me?

Knock, knock.
Who's there?
Izzy.
Izzy who?
Izzy home?

Knock, knock.
Who's there?
Ivan.
Ivan who?
Ivan working
on an invention.

Knock, knock.
Who's there?
Ida.
Ida who?
Ida like to dance to music!

Knock, knock.
Who's there?
Hugo.
Hugo who?
Hugo first, I'll go second.

Knock, knock.
Who's there?
Kim.
Kim who?
Kim too late to the party.

Knock, knock.
Who's there?
Kanye.
Kanye who?
**Kanye make sure
to bring the pizza?**

Knock, knock.
Who's there?
Kent.
Kent who?
**Kent you tell who
I am by my voice?**

Knock, knock.
Who's there?
Jess.
Jess who?
Jess me, myself, and I.

Knock, knock.
Who's there?
Ken.
Ken who?
**Ken you come out
and play with me?**

Knock, knock.
Who's there?
Juno.
Juno who?
**Juno where Europe
is on the map?**

Knock, knock.
Who's there?
Justin.
Justin who?
**Justin the neighborhood
and I thought I'd visit.**

Knock, knock.
Who's there?
Lena.
Lena who?
**Lena little closer and
I'll tell you a secret.**

Knock, knock.
Who's there?
Luke.
Luke who?
**Luke out the window
and you'll see.**

Knock, knock.
Who's there?
Mandy.
Mandy who?
**Mandy lifeboats,
de ship is sinking!**

Knock, knock.
Who's there?
Thermos.
Thermos who?
**Thermos be a better
knock-knock joke
than this!**

Knock, knock.
Who's there?
Marge and Tina.
Marge and Tina who?
**Don't cry for me
Marge and Tina.**

> **Silly Stat:** "Don't Cry
> for Me, Argentina" is a
> show-stopping song about
> Eva Perón's rise
> to power in the movie
> musical *Evita*. Do you
> know who sings it?
> Hint: She also sings the song
> "Like a Prayer."

Knock, knock.
Who's there?
Mikey.
Mikey who?
**Mikey won't fit
in the lock.**

Knock, knock.
Who's there?
Manny.
Manny who?
**Manny people want
to come over.**

Knock, knock.
Who's there?
May.
May who?
May I come in?

Knock, knock.
Who's there?
Nana.
Nana who?
Nana your business.

Knock, knock.
Who's there?
Paul.
Paul who?
**Paul up a chair
and I'll tell you.**

Knock, knock.
Who's there?
Perry.
Perry who?
**Perry well,
and how are you?**

Knock, knock.
Who's there?
Phyllis.
Phyllis who?
**Phyllis in on your
soccer game.**

Knock, knock.
Who's there?
Oliver.
Oliver who?
**Oliver troubles will be
over soon.**

Knock, knock.
Who's there?
Oswald.
Oswald who?
**Oswald my bubble gum.
Ick!**

Knock, knock.
Who's there?
Otto.
Otto who?
**Otto know what's
taking you so long.**

Knock, knock.
Who's there?
Rhoda.
Rhoda who?
**Row, row, Rhoda boat,
gently down the stream ...**

Knock, knock.
Who's there?
Amos.
Amos who?
Amos-quito.

Knock, knock.
Who's there?
Sadie.
Sadie who?
**Sadie magic word
and I'll go away.**

Knock, knock.
Who's there?
Sara.
Sara who?
Sara 'nother way
into this place?

Knock, knock.
Who's there?
Scott.
Scott who?
Scott nothing to do
with you.

Knock, knock.
Who's there?
Seymour.
Seymour who?
Seymour outside if you
open the curtain.

Knock, knock.
Who's there?
Shelby.
Shelby who?
Shelby comin' 'round the
mountain when she comes.

Knock, knock.
Who's there?
Shirley.
Shirley who?
Shirley you can tell
from my voice?

Knock, knock.
Who's there?
Stu.
Stu who?
Stu late, it's time for bed!

Knock, knock.
Who's there?
Troy.
Troy who?
Troy the doorknob.

Knock, knock.
Who's there?
Tyrone.
Tyrone who?
Tyrone shoelaces!

Knock, knock.
Who's there?
Ringo.
Ringo who?
Ringo 'round the rosie.

Knock, knock.
Who's there?
Roland.
Roland who?
A Roland stone
gathers no moss.

Knock, knock.
Who's there?
Theodora.
Theodora who?
Theodora is stuck and
the cat can't get out.

Knock, knock.
Who's there?
Wayne.
Wayne who?
Wayne drops are
falling on my head.

Knock, knock.
Who's there?
Wendy.
Wendy who?
Wendy wind blows,
the cradle will rock.

Silly Stat: In 1936, a newspaper published one of the first knock-knock jokes in print. It was an ad for a new roof. It went like this:

Knock, knock.
Who's there?
Rufus.
Rufus who?
Rufus the most important
part of your house.

Knock, knock.
Who's there?
Tamara.
Tamara who?
Tamara is Monday,
today is Sunday.

Knock, knock.
Who's there?
Will.
Will who?
Will you go to the
party with me?

Knock, knock.
Who's there?
Thea.
Thea who?
Thea tomorrow.

Knock, knock.
Who's there?
Yvonne.
Yvonne who?
Yvonne to be brave!

Knock, knock.
Who's there?
Zach.
Zach who?
Zach's all folks!

Knock, knock.
Who's there?
Mustache.
Mustache who?
I mustache you a question.

Knock, knock.
Who's there?
Amarillo.
Amarillo who?
Amarillo nice gal.

Knock, knock.
Who's there?
Alaska.
Alaska who?
Alaska the questions around here.

Knock, knock.
Who's there?
Candice.
Candice who?
Candice door open?

Knock, knock.
Who's there?
Havana.
Havana who?
Havana wonderful time and wish you were here.

Knock, knock.
Who's there?
Venice.
Venice who?
Venice your mom coming home?

Knock, knock.
Who's there?
Iowa.
Iowa who?
Iowa you a lot of candy!

Silly Stat: In the early part of the twentieth century knock-knock clubs formed in America in the states of Illinois, Iowa, and Kansas.

Knock, knock.
Who's there?
Juneau.
Juneau who?
Juneau what time it is?

Knock, knock.
Who's there?
Oslo.
Oslo who?
**Oslo down so
you can catch up.**

Knock, knock.
Who's there?
Jamaica.
Jamaica who?
Jamaica me a sandwich?

Knock, knock.
Who's there?
Rome.
Rome who?
Rome is where the heart is.

Knock, knock.
Who's there?
Norway.
Norway who?
**There's Norway I'm going
to leave without lunch.**

Knock, knock.
Who's there?
Paris.
*(Try to pronounce this in
French, "Pair-ee!")*
Paris who?
Paris nice to meet you.

Knock, knock.
Who's there?
Al.
Al who?
Al see you in Detroit!

Knock, knock.
Who's there?
Tibet.
Tibet who?
**Early Tibet and
early to rise.**

Knock, knock.
Who's there?
Pakistan.
Pakistan who?
**Pakistan-wich,
you might get hungry.**

Knock, knock.
Who's there?
Tennis.
Tennis who?
Tennis-see.

Knock, knock.
Who's there?
Yukon.
Yukon who?
Yukon say that again.

Knock, knock.
Who's there?
Tunis.
Tunis who?
Tunis company,
three's a crowd.

Knock, knock.
Who's there?
York.
York who?
York on the way home?

Knock, knock.
Who's there?
Mayan.
Mayan who?
Mayan the force
be with you.

Silly Stat: Yoda has three
toes in *The Phantom Menace*.
He's got four in *The Empire
Strikes Back*, *Return of the
Jedi*, and *Revenge of the Sith*.

Knock, knock.
Who's there?
Beth.
Beth who?
Beth wishes for a
happy New Year.

Knock, knock.
Who's there?
Freeze.
Freeze who?
Freeze a jolly good fellow.

Knock, knock.
Who's there?
Eye.
Eye who?
**Eye want to wish you
a happy New Year.**

Knock, knock.
Who's there?
Will.
Will who?
Will you be my Valentine?

Knock, knock.
Who's there?
Irish.
Irish who?
**Irish you a happy
St. Patrick's Day.**

Knock, knock.
Who's there?
Noah.
Noah who?
Noah body! April Fools!

Knock, knock.
Who's there?
Seder.
Seder who?
**Make sure you seder right
story at Passover dinner.**

Knock, knock.
Who's there?
Ana.
Ana who?
Ana-ther Easter bunny.

Knock, knock.
Who's there?
Kenya.
Kenya who?
**Kenya ask Mom for
another potato pancake?**

Silly Stat: Hanukkah,
the Jewish Festival of Lights,
is celebrated on a different
day every year.

Knock, knock.
Who's there?
Berlin.
Berlin who?
**Berlin (*boilin'*) the water
for the Easter eggs.**

Knock, knock.
Who's there?
Carrie.
Carrie who?
**Carrie my Halloween
candy, please.**

Knock, knock.
Who's there?
Bea.
Bea who?
Bea nice to your brother.

Knock, knock.
Who's there?
Bacon.
Bacon who?
**He's bacon brownies
for the bake sale.**

Knock, knock.
Who's there?
Ben.
Ben who?
**Ben waiting all year
for school to end.**

Knock, knock.
Who's there?
Boo hoo.
Boo hoo who?
**Oh, don't cry, it's just
a Halloween costume.**

Knock, knock.
Who's there?
Sasha.
Sasha who?
**Sasha fancy
fireworks display.**

Knock, knock.
Who's there?
Canoe.
Canoe who?
**Canoe watch the Fourth
of July fireworks?**

Knock, knock.
Who's there?
Phillip.
Phillip who?
**Please Phillip my bag
with candy!**

Knock, knock.
Who's there?
Tree.
Tree who?
Tree wise men.

Knock, knock.
Who's there?
Witch.
Witch who?
Witch way to the
haunted house?

Knock, knock.
Who's there?
Wanda.
Wanda who?
Wanda go for a spin
on my broomstick?

Knock, knock.
Who's there?
Witch.
Witch who?
Witch one of you has
the best candy?

Knock, knock.
Who's there?
Esther.
Esther who?
Esther any more
mashed potatoes?

Knock, knock.
Who's there?
Arthur.
Arthur who?
Arthur any more
Thanksgiving leftovers?

Knock, knock.
Who's there?
Dewey.
Dewey who?
Dewey have to wait
long to eat?

Knock, knock.
Who's there?
Eyewash.
Eyewash who?
Eyewash you a
happy Ramadan.

Silly Stat: Ramadan is a month-long time to fast and pray in the Islamic tradition. You can also say, "Ramadan Mubarak," which means "Happy Ramadan" or "Congratulations, it's Ramadan" in Arabic.

Knock, knock.
Who's there?
Annie.
Annie who?
Annie body want some turkey?

Knock, knock.
Who's there?
Anita lift.
Anita lift who?
Anita lift, Rudolph.

Knock, knock.
Who's there?
Honda.
Honda who?
Honda first day of Christmas, my true love sent to me . . .

Knock, knock.
Who's there?
Alaska.
Alaska who?
Alaska Santa for a new bike.

Knock, knock.
Who's there?
Europe.
Europe who?
Europe-ning the door too slowly!

Knock, knock.
Who's there?
Mary.
Mary who?
Mary Christmas.

Knock, knock.
Who's there?
Gladys.
Gladys who?
Gladys Kwanzaa.

Silly Stat: Kwanzaa is a relatively new holiday that began in the United States in 1966 to honor the African-American community after the 1965 Watts riots in Los Angeles. This holiday is centered around the core principles of unity, self-determination, collective work and responsibility, cooperative economics, purpose, creativity, and faith.

Knock, knock.
Who's there?
Holly.
Holly who?
**The Holly-days
are here again!**

Knock, knock.
Who's there?
Harvey.
Harvey who?
**Harvey gonna play
some ball?**

Knock, knock.
Who's there?
Meow.
Meow who?
**Take meow to the
ballgame.**

Knock, knock.
Who's there?
Les.
Les who?
Les go play some golf.

Knock, knock.
Who's there?
Canoe.
Canoe who?
**Canoe play some
video games?**

Knock, knock.
Who's there?
Dozen.
Dozen who?
**Dozen-yone want to
play basketball?**

Knock, knock.
Who's there?
Wanda.
Wanda who?
Wanda play outside?

Knock, knock.
Who's there?
Gargoyle.
Gargoyle who?
**Gargoyle with saltwater
and your throat will
feel better.**

Knock, knock.
Who's there?
Tennis.
Tennis who?
**Tennis my favorite
number.**

Knock, knock.
Who's there?
Uriah.
Uriah who?
Keep Uriah the ball.

Knock, knock.
Who's there?
Wooden shoe.
Wooden shoe who?
**Wooden shoe like
to hear another
knock-knock joke?**

Knock, knock.
Who's there?
Broken pencil.
Broken pencil who?
Never mind, it's pointless.

Knock, knock.
Who's there?
Needle.
Needle who?
**Needle little help
answering the door?**

Knock, knock.
Who's there?
Sherlock.
Sherlock who?
Sherlock your bike.

Knock, knock.
Who's there?
A little old lady.
A little old lady who?
**I didn't know
you could yodel!**

Knock, knock.
Who's there?
Water.
Water who?
**Water you doing
right now?**

Knock, knock.
Who's there?
Lease.
Lease who?
**Lease you could do
is open the door!**

Knock, knock.
Who's there?
Rocket.
Rocket who?
**Rocket-bye baby,
on the treetop . . .**

Knock, knock.
Who's there?
Comb.
Comb who?
Comb on in and sit a bit.

Knock, knock.
Who's there?
Ifor.
Ifor who?
Ifor got!

Knock, knock.
Who's there?
Ima.
Ima who?
Ima make you a snack!

Knock, knock.
Who's there?
Radio.
Radio who?
Radio not, here I come!

Knock, knock.
Who's there?
Cargo.
Cargo who?
Cargo *vroom, vroom.*

Knock, knock.
Who's there?
Howl.
Howl who?
I'm fine, and howl you?

Knock, knock.
Who's there?
Jacken.
Jacken who?
**Jacken Jill went
up the hill.**

Knock, knock.
Who's there?
Tarzan.
Tarzan who?
**Tarzan stripes on the
American flag.**

Knock, knock.
Who's there?
Alien.
Alien who?
**How many aliens
do you know?**

Knock, knock.
Who's there?
Hada.
Hada who?
Hada great time.

Knock, knock.
Who's there?
Bed.
Bed who?
**Bed you can't guess
who this is.**

Knock, knock.
Who's there?
Scold.
Scold who?
**Scold outside.
Put on your jacket!**

Knock, knock.
Who's there?
Althea.
Althea who?
Althea later, alligator.

Knock, knock.
Who's there?
Sir.
Sir who?
**Sir-prise! I have
more jokes for you.**

Tongue Twisters

Tongue twisters serve a practical purpose when practicing pronunciation. (Do you see what I did there?)

They strengthen and stretch the muscles in your mouth and this makes it easier to say some of the toughest sounds. That's why everyone from actors to teachers uses them.

They're also silly. It's fun to challenge yourself, your family, and your friends to see how fast and how many times you can say a tongue twister. Hey, you could even host a Tongue Twist-Off Tournament!

SANTA'S

SHORT

SUIT

SHRUNK

As you practice, here's a trick to be the fastest twister master on your block.

1. Pick a tongue twister.
2. Write it down on a piece of paper.
3. Read it five times to yourself.
4. Whisper it at a normal speed.
5. Now read it out loud, very slowly, five times.
6. Do this again without looking at the paper.

Before you know it, you'll be a tongue twister champion!

Which witch is which?

Shelly shaved six silly sheep.

Toy boat.

Pirates' private property.

Peppered pickles.

Willie's really weary.

Silly superstition.

Right ring, wrong ring.

Eddie edited it.

Six sticky skeletons.

Black back bat.

Rolling red wagons.

She sees cheese.

Quizzical quiz,
kiss me quick.

Cheryl shares
sticky stickers.

Red leather, yellow leather.

Thin sticks, thick brick.

Starred shards of stars.

Pre-shrunk silk shirts.

Sticky tacky cotton candy.

Box of mixed biscuits.

Good blood, bad blood.

Clowns grow
glowing crowns.

When ripe, wipe clean.

Withering weeping
willow tree.

The sushi chef wears
silver socks.

A cement mixer
mixes cement.

Silly Stat: What do all tongue twisters have in common? When certain combinations of sounds are spoken quickly, the speaker loses control of their mouth. The sounds change to mimic each other, for example, "top cop" changes to "top top," and "toy boat" becomes "toy boyt."

Scissors sizzle,
thistles sizzle.

Sheri's horse
houses horseradish.

He threw three free
throws.

Silly Stat: Do you know the human tongue has eight different muscles?

Rubber baby
buggy bumpers.

A big black bear sat on a big black rug.

Tie twine to
three tree twigs.

Tom threw Tim
three thumbtacks.

I eat eel while you peel eel.

Four fine fresh
fish for you.

Eleven benevolent
elephants.

Nine nice night nurses
nursing nicely.

I thought, I thought of
thinking of thanking you.

She sews silvery sweaters
so well.

The queen in
green screamed.

Seth from Sainsbury's
sells thick socks.

Seven slick slimy snakes
slowly sliding southward.

Silly Stat: Did you know that
snakes don't have eyelids?
They have a single scale
over their eye, so it looks
like they sleep with their
eyes open!

A savvy sailor swiftly
sailed his ship into a
slippery slip.

Four frenzied friends
flipped through
their phones.

Double bubble gum,
bubbles double.

The white wagon's round
wonky wheels.

Five frantic frogs fled
from fifty fierce fish.

Roofs of mushrooms rarely
mush too much.

Round and round
the rugged rocks
the ragged rascal ran.

Wayne went to Wales
to watch walruses.

Roberta ran rings around
the Roman ruins.

Six sleek swans swam
swiftly southward.

Silly Stat: Did you know
a male swan is called a
"cob," and a female swan
is called a "pen"?

Clean clams crammed
in clean cans.

I scream, you scream,
we all scream for
ice cream!

Can you can a can as a
canner can can a can?

Andy and Andi-Ann's
anniversary is in April.

I saw a kitten eating
chicken in the kitchen.

Near an ear, a nearer ear,
a nearly eerie ear.

Which wristwatches are
Swiss wristwatches?

I'd rather lather with
lavender soap.

If a dog chews shoes, whose
shoes does he choose?

A sliver of slithering
snake scales.

Don't give crunchy
potato chips to touchy
chinchillas.

Silly Stat: Did you know
it takes four pounds of
raw potatoes to make one
pound of potato chips?

How many saws could a
seesaw saw if a seesaw
could saw saws?

Fuzzy Wuzzy was a bear.
Fuzzy Wuzzy had no hair.
Fuzzy Wuzzy wasn't fuzzy,
was he?

I have got a date at a
quarter to eight. I'll see you
at the gate, so don't be late.

As one blue bug bled black
blood the other black bug
bled blue.

Thirty-three thirsty,
thundering thoroughbreds
thumped Mr. Thurber
on Thursday.

One-One was a racehorse.
Two-Two was one, too.
When One-One won one
race, Two-two
won one, too.

How much wood would
a woodchuck chuck
if a woodchuck could
chuck wood? As much
wood as a woodchuck
would if a woodchuck
could chuck wood.

She sells seashells by the
seashore. And the shells
she sells by the seashore
are seashells for sure.

Silly Stat: The story behind
"She Sells Seashells" is
famous. It is said the rhyme
is about the 19th-century
English paleontologist Mary
Anning. Mary was the first
female fossil hunter thought
to have first discovered
dinosaur bones! She
also identified fossilized
dinosaur poop.

Peter Piper picked a peck
of pickled peppers. A peck
of pickled peppers Peter
Piper picked. If Peter Piper
picked a peck of pickled
peppers, where's the peck
of pickled peppers that
Peter Piper picked?

Silly Stat: Peter and his
famous pickled peppers first
appeared in print in 1813 in
John Harris's *Peter Piper's
Practical Principles of Plain
and Perfect Pronunciation*.

Betty Botter bought some butter. But she said the butter's bitter. If I put it in my batter, it will make my batter bitter. But a bit of bitter butter will make my batter better. So 'twas better Betty Botter bought a bit of bitter butter.

There was a fisherman named Fisher, who fished for some fish in a fissure. 'Til a fish with a grin, pulled the fisherman in. Now they're fishing the fissure for Fisher.

Chester cheetah chews a chunk of cheap Cheddar cheese. If the chunk of cheap Cheddar cheese chunked Chester cheetah, what would Chester cheetah chew on?

Silly Stat: According to researchers at the Massachusetts Institute of Technology (MIT), this is the hardest tongue twister: "Pad kid poured curd pulled cod." According to Guinness World Records, this is the most difficult tongue twister: "The sixth sick sheikh's sixth sheep's sick." Which one gets your vote as the toughest tongue twister?

How many berries could a bare berry carry, if a bare berry could carry berries? Well they can't carry berries (which could make you very wary), but a bare berry carried is more scary!

Silly Sally swiftly shooed seven silly sheep. The seven silly sheep Silly Sally shooed shilly-shallied south.

How much caramel can a cannonball cram in a camel if a cannonball can cram caramel in a camel?

All I want is a proper cup of coffee made in a proper copper coffeepot. I may be off my dot, but I want a cup of coffee from a proper coffeepot. Tin coffeepots and iron coffeepots, they're no use to me. If I can't have a proper cup of coffee in a proper copper coffeepot, I'll have a cup of tea.

I thought a thought. But the thought I thought wasn't the thought I thought I thought. If the thought I thought I thought had been the thought I thought, I wouldn't have thought so much.

Tessie tasted toasty toast, so she could test the toaster. The toaster took toast and toasted it till it was toasty toast.

As he gobbled the cakes on his plate, the greedy ape said as he ate, "The greener green grapes are, the keener keen apes are to gobble green grape cakes, they're great!"

How many cans can a cannibal nibble if a cannibal can nibble cans? As many cans as a cannibal can nibble if a cannibal can nibble cans.

Granny Green grins greatly, gearing up to go gallivanting. Gallivanting gear waits for Granny where she wears her grin.

A tutor who tooted the flute tried to tutor two tooters to toot. Said the two to the tutor, "Is it tougher to toot or to tutor two tooters to toot?"

How much ground would a groundhog hog, if a groundhog could hog ground? A groundhog would hog all the ground he could hog if a groundhog could hog ground.

Through three cheese trees three free fleas flew. While these fleas flew, freezy breeze blew. Freezy breeze made these three trees freeze. Freezy trees made these trees' cheese freeze. That's what made these three free fleas sneeze.

Sheila shares seven shakes with shiny shelled snails
resting on several swaying squashed squares.

How many cookies could a good cook cook, if a good cook could cook cookies? A good cook could cook as many cookies as a good cook who could cook cookies.

> **Silly Stat:** Many sounds use the same muscles, like "c" and "g," or "r" and "w." If you have trouble saying words like "cup" or "cookie," you will probably have trouble with words like "good" and "going."

Of all the felt I ever felt, I never felt a piece of felt which felt as fine as that felt felt when first I felt that felt hat's felt.

Yally Bally had a jolly golliwog. Feeling folly, Yally Bally bought his jolly golli' a dolly made of holly! The golli', feeling jolly, named the holly dolly Polly. So Yally Bally's jolly golli's holly dolly Polly's also jolly!

PUNS

Puns are another kind of joke that juggles word meaning. Sometimes, two words are spelled the same, but the pun plays with their different definitions. Take this one: Broken pencils are pretty *pointless.* Can you think of two meanings for the word "pointless"?

Other times, puns play with words that sound similar but have different meanings, like this: Haunted French pancakes give me the *crepes.* What we really mean is that the haunted French pancake gives us the creeps—yikes! It is funny because crepes are French pancakes.

Puns are clever and they make us think. The more puns you play with, the easier it will be to spot double meanings. In fact, every time you spot a pun, you build on your own *punderful* superpower! Now for some *punny* business . . .

WHEN DO TRUCK DRIVERS STOP TO EAT?

WHENEVER THEY COME TO A

fork

IN THE ROAD.

Every calendar's days are **numbered**.

I tried to catch some fog, but I **mist**.

Velcro—**what a rip off**!

I call my horse Mayo, and sometimes Mayo **neighs**.

Two silk worms had a race. They ended up in a **tie**.

A golf ball is a golf ball no matter how you **putt** it.

Be kind to your dentist; he has **fillings,** too.

Why was Cinderella cut from the soccer team? She ran away from the **ball**.

Venison for dinner again? Oh, **deer**!

Time flies like an arrow. Fruit flies **like** banana.

You can lead a horse to water, but a pencil must be **lead**.

A bicycle can't stand on its own because it is **two-tired**.

I didn't like my beard at first, then it **grew on me**.

Reading while sunbathing makes you well **red**.

Did you hear the joke about peanut butter? I'm not **spreading** it.

A dog had puppies near the road and was ticketed for **littering**.

I did a theatrical performance about puns. It was a **play on words**.

Silly Stat: William Shakespeare, Charles Dickens, Oscar Wilde, and Peggy Parish all liked to use puns in their work. In fact, Shakespeare was a fan of poop puns!

All the toilets in New York's police stations have been stolen. Police have **nothing to go on**.

I used to be a banker, but then I lost **interest**.

I can't believe I got fired from the calendar factory. All I did was take a **day off**.

No matter how much you push the envelope, it'll still be **stationery**.

I thought about becoming a witch, so I tried it for a **spell**.

Broken puppets for sale, **no strings attached**.

Those new corduroy pillows are making **headlines**.

Did you hear about the seafood diet? Every time you **see food,** you eat it!

I was going to look for my missing watch, but I could never **find the time**.

I asked my dad to make me a pair of pants. He was happy to, or at least, **sew it seams**.

Once you've seen
one shopping center
you've **seen a mall**.

Getting paid to sleep
would be a **dream job**.

My fear of moving
stairs is **escalating**.

Do cannibals like to
meat people?

I don't trust these
stairs. They're always
up to something.

Parmesan cheese
is **grate** for you.

Two hats were hanging on a
hat rack in the hallway. One
hat said to the other, "You
stay here; I'll go on **a head**."

A book just fell on my
head. I've only got
my shelf to blame.

When tortilla chips
don't sell fast enough,
the maker knows it will
soon be **crunch** time.

Silly Stat: When there
are pun competitions,
punslingers compete in
rapid-fire duels for the title.
They get a total of five
seconds to come up with
their pun. Whoever runs
out of time or has three
strikes first, loses.

To the guy who invented
zero: Thanks for **nothing**!

I stayed up all night to see
where the sun went, and
then it **dawned** on me.

Inspecting mirrors
is a job I could really
see myself doing.

**Why couldn't
Goldilocks sleep?**
Because she had
night-bears.

Where do sailors take baths?

A *tub-marine*.

What happens when a sea monster gets angry?

It causes a *comm-ocean*.

What do you call a fairy that has not taken a bath?

Stinker Bell.

What's five thousand miles long and purple?

The *grape* wall of China.

Why isn't your nose twelve inches long?

Because then it would be a *foot*.

How do snails fight?

They *slug* it out.

How do bees get to school?

The school *buzzz*.

Why can't chickens play baseball?

Because they hit *fowl* balls.

> **Silly Stat:** Traditional Palestinian weddings have held pun-derful oral poetry duels for hundreds of years.

What did the beach say when the tide finally came in?

Long time, no *sea*.

Why did the pig want to be an actor?

Because he was a real *ham*.

What color socks do bears wear?

They prefer *bare* feet.

What kind of cats like to go bowling?
Alley cats.

Where do butterflies sleep?
On *cater-pillows*.

What do you get when you cross a sea creature and drums?
Fish sticks.

What bird can be heard at mealtimes?
A *swallow*.

What did the doctor prescribe to the sick lemon?
Lemon-*aid*.

What do you call a grumpy cow?
Moooo-dy.

What is the strongest creature in the sea?
A *mussel*.

How do you make an orange laugh?
Tickle its *navel*.

Why did the outlaw rob the bakery?
He *kneaded* the dough.

How do you invite a dinosaur for lunch?
Tea, Rex?

Why did the sheriff go to the barbecue?
He heard it was a place to have a *steak* out.

What do you call a kitten who has sprouted fins and loves to swim?

A *catfish*.

When is music like vegetables?

When you dance to the *beet*.

What fruit never ever wants to be alone?

A *pear*.

What is the craziest, wackiest, most bizarre fruit?

Coconut.

A skeleton walks into a restaurant and places an order for lunch. What is his order?

Spare *ribs*.

What is the musical part of a snake?

The *scales*.

What does a clock do when it's hungry?

It goes back *four seconds*.

Where did the music teacher leave his keys?

On the *piano*.

What do you call an owl that does magic tricks?

Hoo-dini.

What do baseball players eat on?

Home *plates*.

How do turtles talk to each other?
By using *shell* phones.

What did the person who invented the door knocker win?
The No-*bell* prize.

What do you call an academically successful piece of bread?
An honor *roll*.

Silly Stat: Nobel Prize winners are called "laureates," after the Greek laurel wreath given to the best competitors in the olden days. Famous Nobel Prize winners include former U.S. President Barack Obama, who received the Nobel Peace Prize in 2009, and musician Bob Dylan, who received the Nobel Prize in Literature in 2016.

What do you call a pod of musical whales?
An *orca*-stra.

How did dinosaurs decorate their bathrooms?
With rep*tiles*.

What do they call a school with a door made of iron?
The school of *hard knocks*.

How do you know it was an emotional wedding?

The cake was in *tiers*.

What happened to the train driver when he retired?

He got *sidetracked*.

What happened to the guy who got hit in the head with a soda can?

He was lucky it was a *soft* drink.

What happened to the kid who accidentally swallowed some Scrabble tiles?

His next poop could *spell* disaster.

Why do potatoes make good detectives?

Because they keep their *eyes peeled*.

Some guy just threw milk and cheese at me.

How *dairy*!

What do you call a runaway pea?

An *esca-pea*.

What do you call a lazy spud?

A *couch potato*.

What do you call a dinosaur at the rodeo?

A *bronco*-saurus.

Why do magicians do so well in school?

They're good at *trick* questions.

Two vegetarians got into an argument.

Do they still have a *beef* with each other?

What happened when my friend told me he was turning vegan?

I said, "That's a big *missed steak.*"

Why did the guy bring a donkey home?

Because he thought he might get a *kick out of it.*

What happened when I didn't understand math?

My teacher *summed* it up.

What was the reporter doing at the ice cream shop?

Getting the *scoop.*

What happened when I asked the butcher for top-shelf meat?

He said the *steaks were too high.*

Silly Stat: The word "scoop" is used by reporters when they publish an important news story before anyone else. Clare Hollingworth, an English journalist, was the first reporter to break the story about World War II. This was described as "the scoop of the century."

What do you call the father of all sodas?

Pop.

What happens to children who don't pass their coloring exams?

They need a shoulder to *crayon.*

How do sales people approach dinosaurs in clothes shops?

Try, sir, a top?

Why did the spider go to the computer?
To check his *website*.

What happened when I decided I was going to grow some herbs?

I couldn't find the *thyme*.

What happened when the class clown held the door open for me?

I thought it was a nice *jester*.

What do you get from a pampered cow?

Spoiled milk.

What do you call Dracula with hay fever?

The Pollen *Count*.

Silly Stat: Today, humans are better punsters than artificial intelligence (AI). A computer cannot string the words together to form a pun, combine words to make longer ones, or turn verbs into nouns. I guess you could say when it comes to puns, computers *sink* when they think, but humans *sync* when they think.

Why shouldn't you lie to an X-ray technician?

They can *see right through* you.

Have you ever tried to eat a clock?

It's very *time consuming*.

What happens when you sing in the shower and get shampoo in your mouth?

It becomes a *soap opera*.

Where do polar bears vote?

The North *Pole*.

Did you hear about the guy whose whole left side was cut off?

He's all *right* now.

Why are playing cards like wolves?
They come in *packs*.

Why did I burn my Hawaiian pizza today?

I think I should have cooked it on *aloha* temperature.

What do you get if you cross a snake and a LEGO set?

A boa *constructor*.

What do you call a knight who is afraid to fight?

Sir Render.

How do you fix a broken tomato?

With tomato *paste*.

Silly Stat: The origin of the word "surrender" is French and it means to give up. The French famously surrendered during the Battle of Agincourt on October 25, 1415, against the English.

Why are fish so smart?

Because they live in *schools*.

Riddles

Riddles are funny word puzzles that use imagination and humor to solve a problem. When approaching a riddle, be sure to pay close attention to the clues. Remember, you already have all the information you need to figure it out. Have confidence!

Let's try one: I am an odd number. Take away one letter and I become even. What number am I?

All you need to do is look at the sentence from a new angle. Think of the first ten numbers. We can eliminate half of them right away with the information that they are even. That leaves us with, one, three, five, seven, and nine.

Do you see the word "even" in any of these words? If you remove the "s" from seven, what do you have left? The word "even"! You've solved the riddle.

Now you're ready for more riddle detective work . . .

What tells the time but
needs no winding?

A ROOSTER.

What has to be broken
before you can use it?

An egg.

What has hands but
doesn't clap?

A clock.

If a red house is made
of red bricks, and a
yellow house is made of
yellow bricks, what is a
greenhouse made of?

Glass.

What is so fragile that
saying its name breaks it?

Silence.

What goes up but never
comes back down?

Your age.

Zachary's parents
have three sons:
Snap, Crackle, and . . . ?

Zachary.

There are two monkeys
on a tree and one jumps
off. Why does the other
monkey jump, too?

Monkey see, monkey do.

What begins with "t,"
finishes with "t,"
and has tea in it?

A teapot.

You bring me for
dinner but never eat
me, what am I?

A knife and fork.

What has four *i*'s
but can't see?

Mississippi.

What is orange and
sounds like a parrot?

A carrot.

What is easy to get into
but hard to get out of?

Trouble.

What is full of holes but still holds water?

A sponge.

If a father, mother, and their children weren't under an umbrella, why didn't they get wet?

It wasn't raining.

You draw a line. Without touching it, how do you make it a longer line?

Draw a short line next to it and now it's the longer line.

Where does success come before work?

The dictionary.

What has green hair, a round red head, and a long, thin white beard?

A radish.

Where can you find cities, towns, shops, and streets but no people?

A map.

Almost everyone needs it, asks for it, gives it, but almost nobody takes it. What is it?

Advice.

What belongs to you but is used more by others?

Your name.

What has a neck but no head?

A bottle.

What starts with a "p," ends with an "e," and has thousands of letters?

The post office.

What comes once in a minute, twice in a moment, but never in a thousand years?

The letter "m."

What question can you never answer "yes" to?

"Are you asleep?"

I have no feet, no hands, no wings, but I climb the sky. What am I?

Smoke.

Three men were in a boat. It capsized, but only two got their hair wet. Why?

One was bald.

Eric throws a ball as hard as he can. It comes back to him, even though nothing and nobody has touched it. How?

He throws it straight up in the air.

If an electric train is traveling south, which way is the smoke going?

There is no smoke—it is an electric train.

What is next in this sequence? JFMAMJJASON . . .

The letter "D." The sequence contains the first letter of each month.

What is shaped like a box, has no feet, and runs up and down?

An elevator.

What asks no questions but requires many answers?

A doorbell.

How do you spell enemy in three letters?

F-O-E.

Silly Stat: One of Batman's most famous enemies in the comics is The Riddler. His real name is Edward Nygma. Get it?

While looking at a photograph, a man said, "Brothers and sisters have I none. That man's father is my father's son." Who was the person in the photograph?

The man's son.

When is the best time
to have lunch?

After breakfast.

How far is it from
March to June?

A single spring.

What goes up and down
but never moves?

The temperature.

You go into the woods to
get it. Then you sit down
to find it. Then you go
home because you couldn't
find it. What am I?

A splinter.

A queen bee was buzzing,
a worker bee was
buzzing, a honey bee
was buzzing, and a killer
bee was buzzing. How
many b's are in buzzing?

One. There is only one
"b" in "buzzing."

I can run but not walk.
Wherever I go, thought
follows me close
behind. What am I?

A nose.

Why should you always
carry a watch when
crossing a desert?

It has a spring in it.

With what two animals
do most people go to bed?

Two calves.

What has a tongue, but
never talks—has no legs,
but sometimes walks?

A shoe.

When is a bump like a hat?

When it is felt.

What is yellow, looks
like a crescent moon,
and has seeds?

A banana.

The more I appear,
the less you see.
What is it I could be?

Darkness.

When is a door not a door?

When it's ajar.

What is the oldest tree?

The elder.

I'm a container without
hinges, a key, or a lid,
yet golden treasure is
inside. What am I?

An egg.

What is the best thing
to put into pies?

Your teeth.

I am always in front of
you, but you will never
see me. What am I?

The future.

When is a man
like a snake?

When he's rattled.

What has teeth but doesn't
use them for eating?

A comb.

What is the difference
between the North Pole
and the South Pole?

The world.

If snakes marry, what
might their towels say?

Hissss and hers.

What is the last thing
you take off before bed?

Your feet off the floor.

What invention lets you
look right through a wall?

A window.

Name three days
consecutively where
none of the seven days
of the week appear.

Yesterday, today,
and tomorrow.

A man was driving a black truck. His lights were not on. The moon was not out. A lady was crossing the street. How did the man see her?

It was a bright, sunny day.

A doctor and a boy were fishing. The boy was the doctor's son, but the doctor was not the boy's father. Who was the doctor?

His mother.

How do you make the number one disappear?

Add the letter "g" and it's "gone."

What bank never has any money?

The riverbank.

Ms. Blue lives in the blue house, Mr. Pink lives in the pink house, and Mr. Brown lives in the brown house. Who lives in the White House?

The U.S. president.

If you threw a white stone into the Red Sea, what would it become?

Wet.

What has four legs, but can't walk?

A table.

In a one-story pink house, there was a pink person, a pink cat, a pink fish, a pink computer, a pink chair, a pink table, a pink telephone, a pink shower—everything was pink! What color were the stairs?

There are no stairs. It's a one-story house.

I have keys but no locks. I have space but no room. You can enter but can't go outside. What am I?

A computer keyboard.

How do you spell "cow" in 11 letters?

SEE-O-DOUBLE-U.

I am not alive, but I grow. I've got no lungs, but I need air.
I don't have a mouth, but water drowns me. What am I?

Fire.

What animal grows down as it grows up?

A goose.

How far can a fox run into the woods?

Only halfway, otherwise it would be running out of the woods.

What is bought by the yard and worn by the foot?

Carpet.

I make a loud noise when I am changing. I get lighter as I get bigger. What am I?

Popcorn.

What does a cat have that no other animal has?

Kittens.

I can be any color you can imagine. You see me in everyday life. I've been around for many years. If you look around you can probably see some of me right now. What am I?

Paint.

A monkey, a squirrel, and a bird are racing to the top of a coconut tree. Who will get the banana first?

None of them. You can't get a banana from a coconut tree!

I am a number with a couple of friends; quarter a dozen, and you'll find me again. What am I?

Three.

Silly Stat: The word dozen means a group of 12. A "baker's dozen" means one more than the standard 12. So, when you buy bagels, ask for a baker's dozen and you'll get 13!

If there are four apples and you take away three, how many do you have?

You took three apples, so you have three.

How many times can you subtract the number five from 25?

Once, because after you've subtracted five, it's no longer the number 25.

Which month has 28 days?

All of them, of course!

If two's company and three's a crowd, what are four and five?

Nine.

What has a thumb and four fingers, but is not alive?

A glove.

What's the easiest way to double your money?

Fold it in half.

When you have me, you feel like sharing me. But if you share me you don't have me. What am I?

A secret.

What weighs more, a pound of iron or a pound of feathers?

Both would weigh the same. A pound is a pound.

If a rooster laid 13 eggs and the farmer took eight of them and then another rooster laid 12 eggs and four of them were rotten, how many of the eggs were left?

Roosters don't lay eggs.

Two fathers and two sons sat down to eat eggs for breakfast. They ate exactly three eggs, each person had an egg. Explain how they did it.

One of the fathers is also a grandfather. Therefore, one father is both a son and a father. That makes three people, so each got an egg.

Laura has four daughters, each of her daughters has a brother, how many children does Laura have?

Five, each daughter has the same brother.

What tastes better than it smells?

A tongue.

How many letters are there in the English alphabet?

18: three in "the," seven in "English," and eight in "alphabet."

Throw away the outside and cook the inside, then eat the outside, and throw away the inside. What is it?

Corn on the cob. You throw away the husk, cook and eat the kernels, and throw away the cob.

Take off my skin, I won't cry, but you will. What am I?

An onion.

How can a leopard change its spots?

By moving from one spot to another.

I am a seed with three
letters in my name.
Take away two letters
and I sound quite the
same. What am I?

A pea.

I am a bird, I am a
fruit, and I am a
person. What am I?

A Kiwi.

A one-seeded fruit I
may be, but all of your
calendars are full of
me. What am I?

Dates.

I have wings and I have
a tail, across the sky
is where I sail. Yet I
have no eyes, ears, or
mouth. What am I?

A kite.

She's the head of a hive.
On a chessboard, she is
seen. She's in a deck of
cards. Who could she be?

A queen.

It is there from the very
start and will be there
until the end. To end
you must cross over.
And you must pass
through it to begin.

The finish line.

I go around and round,
with no beginning and
no end. What am I?

A doughnut.

Your mother and father
have a child. It's not
your brother and not
your sister. Who is it?

You.

What is often on the
ground getting stepped on
by others, but you don't
have to wash it because
it never gets dirty; in
fact, you couldn't wash
it even if you tried?

A shadow.

I am beautiful, up in the sky. I am magical, yet I cannot fly. To some people, I bring luck; to some people, riches. The person at my end does whatever he wishes. What am I?

A rainbow.

Reaching stiffly for the sky, I bare my fingers when it's cold. In warmth, I wear an emerald glove and in between, I dress in gold. What am I?

A tree.

What lives without a body, hears without ears, speaks without a mouth, to which the air alone gives birth?

An echo.

My feet stay warm, but my head is cold. No one can move me, I'm just too old. What am I?

A mountain.

Built of metal or wood to divide. It will make us good neighbors, if you stay on your side. What is it?

A fence.

WAIT FOR IT . . .

Welcome to jokes with a longer setup. How do longer jokes work?

Read the stories below and make them yours. Take the time to learn them, so you can tell them as if they happened to you. Remember to pace yourself so your audience eagerly anticipates the punchline. Have them perched on the edge of their seats, then . . . deliver it!

Use longer jokes around the campfire, at home, in the car, or whenever you feel like telling a story or taking the stage!

A DUCK WADDLES INTO THE GROCERY STORE TO BUY A CAN OF SODA. THE CLEARK LOOKS DOWN AT HIM AND ASKS, "WOULD YOU LIKE TO PAY WITH CASH OR CREDIT?" THE DUCK REPLIES, "JUST PUT IT ON MY BILL."

David is hungry and stops at the local restaurant for a bowl of soup. The waiter brings it over and places it on the table in front of him. David's stomach rumbles with hunger. He picks up his spoon, excited to take his first bite, when he freezes. Nestled among the tasty noodles is a fly. "Waiter!" he calls. The waiter rushes over. "Yes?" "What is this fly doing in my soup?" The waiter leans over, his nose almost touching the bowl, and replies, "The backstroke."

Two fleas go to the movies. When they get out, they stand for a while in the traffic. All around them people are rushing, horns are blaring. One flea turns to the other and asks, "Do you want to walk or should we take a dog home?"

Two knives are side by side in the silverware drawer. One knife turns to the other and says, "You're looking sharp!"

Jason stands nervously before the teacher. "Would I get in trouble for something I didn't do?" Mrs. Roberts replies, "Of course not." "Good," Jason says. "Because I didn't do my homework."

A young boy knocks on the door on Halloween night and says, "Trick or treat?" The woman opens the door and looks at him. After a few seconds, she says, "I don't know if I can give you a treat. What are you supposed to be?" "A werewolf," the boy answers. The woman shakes her head. "But you're not wearing a costume. You've only got your normal clothes on." With a laugh, the boy replies, "Well, it's not a full moon yet, is it?"

Alex looks very sad, so his friend Saeed asks him what is wrong. "I lost my dog today," Alex says. Saeed nods, "That's too bad. Hey, why don't you put an ad in the paper?" Alex thinks about it for a bit then shakes his head. "What good would that do? My dog can't read."

A boy asks his father, "Dad, are bugs good to eat?" "Son, please don't talk about things like that over dinner," the dad replies. After dinner the father asks, "Now, son, what did you want to ask me?" "Oh, nothing," the boy says. "There was a bug in your soup, but you ate it."

The teacher says to the class, "A man rode his horse to town on Friday. The very next day he rode back on Friday. How is this possible?" Keisha raises her hand and says, "The horse's name was Friday."

"Yuki, why is your little sister crying?" Mom asks her son, while watching her daughter sob with dismay. Yuki shrugs and replies, "Because I helped her." Mom relaxes back into her seat with a relieved smile. "But that's a good thing! What did you help her with?" she asks proudly as her daughter wails loudly. Yuki says, "I helped her eat the rest of her gummy bears."

"I'm the fastest animal in the jungle," the lion roars. The cheetah shakes her head. "I don't think so. Let's race and see." The whole population of the jungle shows up. Elephants stand next to gazelles. Rhinos and hippos line up. Hyenas and zebras and every other animal wait to see the outcome of the race. The lion is very confident he will win. The race begins and the cheetah takes off. She wins by a mile and is declared the fastest animal in the jungle. The lion is embarrassed and can't believe he lost. "You're a cheater!" he shouts. "Yep, and you're a lion," the cheetah replies.

Jennifer goes to visit her friend and is amazed to find her playing chess with her dog. The little Shih Tzu sits on a cushion, and Jennifer watches with fascination as the dog's little front paw accurately moves the pieces around the board. "I can hardly believe my eyes!" Jennifer exclaims in astonishment. Her friend waves her hand in dismissal. "Oh, she's not so smart. I've beaten her three games out of five."

A bear walks into a coffee shop and tells the barista, "I'll have a latte . . . . with extra foam." The barista replies, "What's with the big pause?" The bear looks at his paws and replies, "I don't know, my dad has them, too."

Arjun holds up his smartphone. "I had to take my phone to the dentist yesterday." "Really, why?" says Gabi. Arjun answers, "Because it had a Bluetooth."

"Jada, why can't dinosaurs clap?" Jada thinks for a minute and says, "Because they're extinct!"

Mr. Noah goes in for a very special surgery on his hands. The doctor tells him how complicated it will be. Mr. Noah holds up his hands and says, "Doctor, will I be able to play piano once you are done?" The doctor nods. "Of course!" "That's good," Mr. Noah replies. "Because I've always wanted to play the piano."

"I'm the fastest animal in the jungle," the lion roars. The cheetah shakes her head. "I don't think so. Let's race and see." The whole population of the jungle shows up. Elephants stand next to gazelles. Rhinos and hippos line up. Hyenas and zebras and every other animal wait to see the outcome of the race. The lion is very confident he will win. The race begins and the cheetah takes off. She wins by a mile and is declared the fastest animal in the jungle. The lion is embarrassed and can't believe he lost. "You're a cheater!" he shouts. "Yep, and you're a lion," the cheetah replies.

Elijah sits glumly on the porch, his hand holding his chin. Stuart rides by on his bike and sees his friend deep in thought. He jumps off and puts his bike against the fence. "Hey, Elijah. What's bothering you, buddy?" "Oh, I heard a funny joke about a boomerang earlier, and I've forgotten it." "Don't worry about it," Stuart tells him. "I'm sure it will come back to you eventually."

I like Northern and Eastern European food, so I decided to Russia over there because I was Hungary. After Czeching the menu, I ordered Turkey, with a Danish. When I was Finnished, I told the waiter, "It's all good, but there is Norway I could eat another bite."

David goes back the next day. He gets the same waiter and again looks down into his bowl of soup and sees another fly! "Waiter," he cries out. "There's another fly in my soup." The waiter walks over to peer down. He looks at the rest of the table and says, "Don't worry, sir, the spider from the bread roll will get him."

David has just about had it with this restaurant, but he gives it one last try. "Waiter," he asks. "Can I have cold mashed potatoes, burnt chicken, and a wilted salad?" The waiter gives him a funny look and replies, "No, we don't serve food like that here." David smiles and says, "You did the last time I was here."

Diego walks up to his mother and says, "Mom, all the kids at school make fun of me." His mother asks, "Why, sweetie?" Diego replies, "Well, Mom, all the other students say I'm a werewolf." She pats him on the head and says, "Don't worry honey, just remember at nighttime to comb all your fur to the right side."

A man gets his house painted. When the painters are finished, they hand him the bill. He is surprised to find that the painters have not charged him for paint, just for painting. He asks them, "You did a great job, but why didn't you charge me for paint, too?" The painter replies, "Don't worry about the paint, sir. It's on the house."

An ant and a centipede are hanging out and having a great time. After an hour or so, they run out of food. The ant decides to go out and get more, but the centipede tells him, "Let me go, I'm faster with all of my legs." The ant says, "You're right about that. Okay, you go." The ant waits and waits. After a couple of hours, he wonders where the centipede is, and calls. "What's taking so long?" he asks impatiently. The centipede replies, "Hold on, I almost have all my shoes on."

Finding one of his students making faces at others on the playground, Mr. Mason stops to gently reprimand the child. Smiling kindly, the teacher says, "Johnny, when I was a little boy, I was told that if I made faces, my face would freeze like that." Little Johnny looks up and replies, "Well, Mr. Mason, you can't say you weren't warned."

Mr. P. doesn't like to spend money, but his husband and daughter convince him to go out for dinner. He reluctantly agrees to go to a local restaurant. When he enters the restaurant, he asks the host, "How are your prices?" The host replies, looking at the man's daughter, "Well, kids eat free." Mr. P. replies, "In that case, my daughter is really hungry. She's going to have three plates."

Gabe is sitting at home when he hears a knock at the door. He opens the door and sees a tiny snail on the porch. He picks up the snail and throws it as far as he can. A year later, there's a knock at the door. Gabe opens it and sees the same snail. The snail looks up at him and says, "What was that all about, man?"

On a hot day in August, a mailman pauses by an old house where a painter is busy painting it from top to bottom. The painter is dripping with sweat. He is wearing a heavy parka as if it were the middle of the winter. The postman walks up to the mailbox, and to his surprise, he realizes the painter has another jacket on underneath the opened parka. The puzzled mailman says, "It's kind of hot today." "Sure is," says the painter, who pauses to take a long drink of water and wipe his brow. The mailman points to the painter. "Why are you wearing those parkas, then?" The painter holds up the paint can he is using and shows the mailman the instructions. "Says right here, 'For best results, put on two coats.'"

Kayla goes with her dad to pick up fruit and vegetables at a local farm. It is hot outside and she notices a boy scratching his foot in the dirt. He bobs his head and says, "Cluck, cluck, cluck." Kayla jumps back in shock. "Why is that boy saying, 'Cluck, cluck, cluck,' and scratching in the dirt?" The mother of the boy is stocking produce in the bins. "Oh, he thinks he's a chicken." Kayla shakes her head. "Well, why don't you tell him he's not a chicken?" The boy's mother looks around to see if anybody is listening. She leans closer to Kayla and whispers, "Well, we need the eggs."

A woman is driving a truck down the road when a policeman hails her down. In the rear of the truck are a gaggle of penguins. The policeman walks up to the truck and asks, "What are you doing with all these penguins?" "These are my penguins," the woman replies. "They belong to me." "You need to take them to a zoo," the policeman insists. The driver nods and says, "Will do." The next day, at the same time, and at the same intersection, the policeman sees the truck filled with penguins. He halts the driver and says, "I thought I told you to take these penguins to the zoo." The woman nods. "I did," she says calmly. "And today, I'm taking them to the movies."

Three friends are stranded on a desert island. All they want is to go home, but no ships have passed by and they are quite alone in the middle of nowhere. One day, one of them digs a hole and, to his surprise, pulls out a lamp. "Maybe it's a magic lamp. Rub it and let's see if a genie appears!" one of the men shouts. The man who found it gently wipes the grit from the lamp and, to his astonishment, smoke pours from the spout to curl around their heads. "Holy cow! That's a real genie," he cries. "Yes," the deep voice fills the air. "I will grant you three wishes. Remember to use them wisely. There will be only three wishes allowed." One of the friends rushes forward and shouts, "I want to go home, now!" The genie snaps his fingers and the first friend vanishes in a puff of purple smoke. "I want to go home, too," the second friend proclaims. In an instant, he, too, is gone. The third man looks at the empty island and the blue expanse of the sea. He hears nothing but the cry of the seagulls and the crash of the waves. He swallows a sob and says, "I sure am lonely. I wish I had my friends back."

Grandpa is very grumpy. He stomps around the house with a scowl on his face. "Gramps," his granddaughter asks. "Is your foot bothering you?" He shakes his head, "Nah. Gout is under control right now." "Don't you like your new cane?" "What, this thing?" He holds up the walking stick. "It's fine." "Then what is it?" Grandpa sighs and points to the steps going upstairs. "It's the chairlift your father installed—the darn thing is driving me up a wall!"

Robert breaks both of his arms in an accident, so he has to wear a cast on each arm from wrist to elbow. Eventually, with his two casts, he takes a walk and pauses outside of a music shop. In the window is the most beautiful guitar he has ever seen. He stares at it for a long time, shakes his head, and walks through the door. "How much is that guitar?" He nods toward the instrument. "That one? It's very expensive," the owner responds. "I don't care! I'm going to buy it." The owner looks at the guitar and at Robert's two casts. "How will you use it?" Robert smiles. "I'll just play it by ear."

A kangaroo and rabbit are sitting together in the brush watching their offspring. "Oh, no," the kangaroo moans. "What's wrong?" The rabbit pauses from eating her carrot. "It's the forecast. It's calling for rain." The rabbit sniffs the air a bit. "That's okay. We could use the water." "Sure." The kangaroo pats her pouch. "But that means my kids will have to play inside all day."

One day a man with an elephant walks into a movie theater. "I'm afraid I can't let your elephant in here, sir," the manager says. "Oh, don't worry. He's very well behaved," the man says. "All right, then," the manager says. "If you're sure . . ." After the movie, the manager says to the man, "I'm very surprised! Your elephant was so well behaved, and he even seemed to enjoy the movie!" "Yes, I was surprised, too," says the man. "Especially since he wasn't a fan of the book."

A chicken marches into the library, walks up to the library desk and says, "Book, book, BOOK!" The librarian hands over a couple of thin paperbacks and watches the chicken leave the library, walk across the street, through a field, and disappear down a hill. The next day, the chicken is back. It walks right up to the librarian, drops the books on her desk, and says, "Book, Book, BOOK, BOOK!" The librarian hands over a few more books and watches the chicken drag them away. The next day, the chicken comes for a third time, and once again goes through the same routine. This time, once the chicken is out the door, the librarian follows—across the street, through a field, and down the hill to a small pond. On a rock at the edge of the pond is the biggest frog the librarian has ever seen. The chicken walks up to the frog, drops the book on the pond's edge, and says, "Book, Book, Book!" The frog hops over, uses its front leg to push through the pile, and says: "Read it, read it, read it."

Four boys were late for school, so the teacher asks one of them, "Ryan, why were you late?" Ryan responds, "Because, my clock was 15 minutes late." Next the teacher asks, "Garrett, why were you late?" Garrett answers, "Because my tires were flat." The teacher then asks, "Scott, why were you late?" Scott belches and says, "I ate too much this morning, so I walked slowly to school." After Scott finishes, Jack starts to cry. The teacher asks, "Why are you crying, Jack? I didn't even ask you yet." Jack replies, "They used up all my excuses."

Howie visits his 90-year-old grandpa who lives way out in the country. On the first morning of the visit, Howie's grandpa prepares a breakfast of bacon and eggs. Howie notices a filmy substance on his plate and asks, "Are these plates clean, Gramps?" His grandpa replies, "They're as clean as cold water can get them. Just go ahead and finish your meal." For lunch, Grandpa makes hamburgers. Again, Howie is concerned about the plates. His has specks of dried egg on it. "Are you sure these plates are clean?" he asks, flaking off the dried food. Without looking up, Grandpa says, "I told you before, those dishes are as clean as cold water can get them!" Later, as Howie is leaving, his grandpa's dog won't let him pass. Howie says, "Gramps, your dog won't let me walk by him." Grandpa yells to the dog, "Cold Water, go lie down!"

Anton comes running into the house. "Mom, there's a man outside with a broken arm named Sheldon." "Well," says Mom. "That's a funny name for a broken arm!"

A jockey is about to enter a race on a new horse. The horse's trainer meets him before the race and says, "All you have to remember with this horse is that every time you approach a jump, you have to shout, 'ALLLEEEY-OOOP!' really loudly in the horse's ear. As long as you do that, you'll be fine." The jockey thinks the trainer is little bit wacky, but promises to shout those words. The race begins and they approach the first hurdle. The jockey ignores the trainer's silly advice and the horse crashes straight through the center of the jump. They keep going and approach the second hurdle. The jockey, somewhat embarrassed, whispers "Alley-oop" in the horse's ear. The same thing happens—the horse crashes straight through the center of the jump. At the third hurdle, the jockey thinks, "It's no good, I'll have to do it," and yells, "ALLLEEEY-OOOP!" really loudly. Sure enough, the horse sails over the jump with no problem. This continues for the rest of the race, but due to the earlier crashes, the horse only finishes third. The trainer asks the jockey what went wrong. The jockey replies, "Nothing is wrong with me—it's this horse. What, is he deaf or something?" The trainer replies, "Deaf? He's not deaf. He's blind!"

A young boy has a dream of being in a circus. He approaches the manager of the circus and tells him, "I can do the best bird impression you have ever seen." The manager says, "That's nothing special, a lot of people can do bird impressions." The boy turns to him and says, "Okay." Then he flaps his arms and flies away.

Rebecca's teacher asks her, "If I give you two cats, then two more, and two more cats, how many do you have?" Rebecca calls out, "Seven!" The teacher looks at her and asks more slowly, "If I give you two cats, then two more, and two more cats, how many do you have?" Rebecca repeats, "Seven!" Next, the teacher asks, "If I get two cats, then two more, and two more cats, how many would I have?" Rebecca responds, "Six!" "Good job, Rebecca!" To make sure she really understands, the teacher says, "Now, if I give you two cats, then two more, and two more cats, how many do you have?" Rebecca thinks for a second, "Seven." Her teacher says, "Rebecca, where do you keep getting seven cats from?" Rebecca answers, "You keep giving me six cats, and I already have a cat!"

An elderly woman burst into a pet store. "I want to buy a canary, but it's got to be a good singer." The shop owner begins moving a ladder toward a small cage on a shelf about 15 feet up, near the ceiling of the store. "Ma'am, I've been in this business for 40 years and the best singer I've ever heard is in that cage." "Don't think I'm going to pay a pretty penny just because you are climbing that ladder. It's got to be a singer!" By this point, the shopkeeper is coming down the ladder. "Ma'am, this bird is pretty much a canary Justin Bieber." The bird opens its beak and sings a beautiful tune. Awed, the woman murmurs, "Why, he *is* a good singer." She takes a good look at the bird, her eyes narrowed. "Hey, this bird has only got one leg!" The pet store owner replies, "Do you want a singer or a dancer?"

David goes back to that same restaurant, sits at his usual table, and orders the usual—soup. The waiter sets it down in front of him and says, "No fly!" Then he stands back to watch him eat it. But David just sits there. "Is there something wrong?" the waiter asks. "I can't eat this soup," David replies. "Is it too hot?" the waiter asks. "Nope." "Too cold?" David shakes his head. The waiter calls for the owner and the chef, and each goes through the same routine: "Too hot?" "Too cold?" "No, no . . . No, no." Finally, the chef, at his wit's end, says, "Sir, I will taste the soup myself. Where is the spoon?" David says, "Aha!"

A struggling zoo's main attraction, a gorilla, gets sick during their most popular season. They can't afford to lose the gorilla, so they secretly hire one of the employees to be a gorilla in a suit for an extra $200 a week. The gorilla-man quickly becomes even more popular than the original gorilla. After a few months, he gets less popular, so the gorilla-man decides to raise the stakes. He climbs out of his pen and dangles from a tree in the lion exhibit, but he loses his grip and falls. Scared, he begins to yell for help, "Somebody help!" With this, the lion pounces on top of him and whispers, "Quiet, or you'll get us both fired!"

A pirate walks into a bar with an eye patch, a peg leg, and a hook for a hand. The bartender notices his leg. "How did you get that peg leg?" The pirate replies, "It were many years ago. I were walkin' on the deck when a wave swept a shark aboard. The shark bit off me leg!" "Wow," replies the bartender. "What about that hand?" The pirate nods. "It were many years ago. I were walkin' on the deck when a wave swept a killer whale aboard. The whale bit me bloomin' hand off!" "Oh," says the bartender. "How about the eye?" The pirate replies, "It were many years ago. I were walkin' on the deck when a seagull came outta nowhere and pooped in me eye." "And that blinded you?" asked the bartender. "No, 'twas my first day with the hook."

A man walks into a coffee shop with his dog, but the barista says, "You can't bring your dog in here." The man responds, "This is no ordinary dog. You see, my dog can talk. I'll prove it to you. Sparky, what covers trees?" The dog replies, "Bark!" Next, the man asks, "What's on top of a house?" Sparky answers, "Roof!" Finally, the man asks, "Who's your favorite baseball player?" The dog says, "Ruth!" The barista immediately throws them both out. The man says, "Sheesh, what was that guy's problem?" The dog answers, "Maybe he's not a Yankees fan."

A girl walks into a fancy restaurant and says to the owner, "If you give me free food all night, I will entertain your customers and they will spend lots of money on food all night." "Oh yeah?" says the owner. "How are you going to do that?" The girl gets a hamster out of her pocket and puts it on the piano. The hamster runs up and down the keyboard playing the greatest piano music anyone had ever heard. "That's incredible!" says the owner. "Have you got anything else?" The girl gets a parrot out of her other pocket and puts it on top of the piano. The hamster begins to play the piano again and the parrot sings along. Everyone in the restaurant is amazed and stays all night eating and listening to the hamster and parrot. The owner is delighted. "I must have these animals. Will you sell them to me?" he asks. The girl shakes her head. "Will you sell just one then?" asks the owner. "Okay, I'll sell you the parrot for $100," the girl says. The owner of the restaurant is delighted and hands over the money. Another patron standing next to the girl says, "Don't you think that's quite cheap for such a clever parrot?" "Not at all," the girl replies. "The hamster is a ventriloquist!"

A man goes into a pet shop to buy a parrot. The shop owner points to three identical looking parrots on a perch and states, "The parrot on the left costs $1,000." "Why does that parrot cost so much?" asks the man. The owner says, "Well, that parrot knows how to use a computer." The man then asks about the next parrot. "Oh, that one is $1,500. Not only does it know how to use a computer, but it knows how to program." He points to the third bird on the perch. "That one is $5,000." "What can it do?" The owner shrugged, "To be honest, I have never seen it do a thing, but the other two call him 'boss'!"

Two Inuit huddle in a kayak. It is bitterly cold, and they are far from home. One of them gets the idea to light a fire in the narrow boat. Within minutes, it sinks, proving once again that you can't have your kayak and heat it, too.

A cruise ship passes by a remote island in the Pacific Ocean. The passengers cluster on the deck to see a bearded man running around and waving his arms wildly. "Captain," one passenger asks, "who is that man over there?" "I have no idea," the captain says, "but he goes nuts every year when we pass him."

A couple is sitting inside by the fire when the radio announcer comes on: *"We are expecting up to a foot of snow tonight, so please make sure you are parked on the even-numbered side of the road."* The husband goes out and moves their car. The next day, the same thing happens and the announcer comes on: *"We are expecting up to a foot of snow tonight, please make sure you are parked on the odd-numbered side of the road."* Again, the man goes out and moves the car. A few days later the same thing happens and the announcer says: *"We are expecting up to two feet of snow tonight, please make sure you are parked on the—"* But the power goes out in the middle of the announcement. The husband starts panicking. "Which side do I put our car on?" His wife looks up from her newspaper and replies, "How about we just leave the car in the garage this time?"

Your Turn

Humor is portable and travels light. You don't even need a suitcase to take it with you.

This area is a place for you to write down your own jokes, and to learn to make jokes just by paying closer attention to the world around you.

Let's get crackin'.

Tip #1:

Did you hear, see, touch, taste, or smell something funny recently? Jot it down!

Tip #2:

Comics sometimes take two ideas and bring them together. Can you think of two jokes you've read and combine them into one?

Tip #3:

A series of jokes is called a "set." A good comedian
starts with a joke about one subject and brings
it full circle to end their set with a similar joke.
What will your first set begin and end with?
(Maybe an animal or your favorite food?)

Tip #4:

Try creating jokes by finding something funny in your house. For example, can you think of something funny related to eggs?

Question: Where's Eddie?
Answer 1: He cracked under pressure.
Answer 2: He's been poached.

(Hey, this is no yolk!)

Tip #5:

Take three words and let's see if you can put them into knock-knock jokes.

Knock, knock.
Who's there?
Goat.
Goat who?

Goat _____

Knock, knock.
Who's there?
Stopwatch.
Stopwatch who?

Stopwatch _____

Knock, knock.
Who's there?
Dragon.
Dragon who?

Dragon _____

If you put some thought into anything, you can turn it into a yolk . . . I mean a joke.

Why did the chicken cross the road?

(Hint: You know this one!)

What did one wall say to the other wall?

(Hint: Where do two walls meet?)

Where do cows go for entertainment?

(Hint: Think about what a cow says!)

What animal needs to wear a wig?

(Hint: What bird has nothing on top of its head?)

Why are elephants so wrinkled?

(Hint: How do you get wrinkles out of clothing?)

What's green and can fly?

(Hint: Use your imagination here!)

About the Author

CAROLE P. ROMAN is the award-winning author of more than 50 children's books. Whether about pirates, princesses, or discovering the world around us, her books have enchanted educators, parents, and her diverse audience of children. She hosts a blog radio program and is one of the founders of a new magazine, *Indie Author's Monthly*.

CPSIA information can be obtained
at www.ICGtesting.com
Printed in the USA
LVHW022329130220
646585LV00002B/2